INSIGHTS

Concise and thoughtful Jewish wisdom

Rabbi Benjamin Blech

Rabbi Benjamin Blech is a Professor of Talmud at Yeshiva University and an internationally recognized educator, religious leader, author, and lecturer. A recipient of the American Educator of the Year award and author of twelve highly acclaimed books, he writes regularly for major newspapers and journals and was recently ranked #16 in a listing of the 50 most influential Jews in America.

Introduction

So many books – so little time.

The hurried pace of our lives, the all-consuming demands of our daily activities, the stresses of our struggle for simple survival leave us most often unable to pursue in any really meaningful way the answers to the very profound questions that define our existence and our purpose on Earth.

Most people just don't have the opportunity to study in depth the scholarly works of the greatest minds of the past that help us in our quest to really understand the meaning of our lives.

That's why I've made this effort to offer a series of short insights into some of the most fundamental subjects of interest to anyone concerned with living a life that is spiritually ennobling, personally fulfilling and blessed with achievements that leave the world enriched by our presence.

I hope the pages that follow will justify the profound observation of Chief Justice Oliver Wendell Holmes that "a moment's insight is sometimes worth a life's experience."

* * *

Self

A Different Life

If God created us, there must be a special reason why we've been placed here on Earth. What is our purpose?

It may seem strange at first to put it this way but the purpose of every one of us is to be different – different at least in some special way from everyone else.

How do I know that?

Jewish philosophers stress an idea that is common to many other religions. Since God represents the greatest good and the essence of our loftiest ideals, we are obligated above all to imitate Him. Being like God best summarizes our spiritual aspiration.

Christians share this concept and refer to it with the Latin phrase *imitatio dei.*

And what do we identify as the single most important thing we know about God?

It is the idea expressed in the catechism of the Jew, recited every morning and evening. "Hear O Israel, the Lord is our God, *the Lord is one*".

God is one.

Rabbi Soloveitchik, my teacher and one of the greatest Jewish scholars of the past generation, offered a profound interpretation of this phrase. In Hebrew, "one" doesn't simply refer to the first number. It can be translated in another way. One means unique. One refers to an object or person that is different, that stands alone, or – perhaps better put – that is outstanding.

What is most impressive about God is quite simply that He is unique.

Now we can understand in a far more profound way the obligation imposed upon us to be like Him.

When He created every one of us, He created us to be unique and different. There is no other *me* on this earth, the same way there is no other *you*.

We often hear a phrase that ought to be banned for religious reasons.

We speak of the average person. There is no average person. We cannot be average if by average we mean be like everyone else. That voids our very reason for being.

The very fact of our creation implies a unique purpose. Our first step in fulfilling it is to acknowledge that God obviously thought there was good reason for Him to put us here on Earth. Our next step is to discover what makes us special – and then to fulfill our potential, which was the reason for having been created.

Free Will

According to Maimonides, the most important idea in Judaism is free will.

The rabbis of the Talmud expressed a very daring concept: human beings are greater than Angels.

How can that possibly be? Angels are perfect while human beings often fall short of their spiritual obligations?

The answer is simple: Angels are perfect because they have no choice. They are basically robots, fulfilling their divine missions as automatons. They deserve no credit for doing what they are pre-programmed to do.

Human beings are different. We have been given free will. That makes our sins possible but also turns our good deeds into noble achievements, the results of our free-willed choice to overcome the seductive call of our baser instincts.

Anyone who studies the Bible understands this. That is why the Bible promises reward for the righteous even as it warns of punishment for the wicked.

Free will works within the context of certain conditions.

Obviously, I understand that you are not as free to do many things if you are born into poverty rather than into wealth. But morally and ethically you are just as free.

Consider the people who have reached great heights in many different professions as well as those renowned for major achievements. They come from all environments, economic strata, and environments. How can that be? Because we are free to become great even if we, like Helen Keller for example, are saddled with the greatest disabilities.

Free choice is why God in the Bible says to every one of us, "Behold, I give before you life or death, good and evil. Choose life."

You have the ability to choose – and that's what makes you greater than Angels.

Creativity

In most religions, particularly in Judaism, there is a master *mitzvah* (commandment), as I've already mentioned, to imitate God.

What is the very first thing that we know about God, from the first verse of the Bible?

"In the beginning God created the heavens and the earth." God created the world. God is a creator. And when He created us, He said, "I want you to be like me."

What does that mean? In which way can we be most like Him?

By being creators.

In the simplest sense, by being fruitful and multiply, we continue to procreate the world. But Jewish philosophers teach us that becoming creators like God means much more.

In a fascinating phrase in the Talmud we are told, "The role of human beings is *to be partners with God in the creation of the world.*"

God left the world unfinished. And that's because he wanted to leave room for us to join Him in the sacred task of perfecting the world.

God created the world in seven days and then, on the first Saturday night, He gave us the power of fire. With fire mankind learnt to harness the powers of nature. With fire we were able to forge tools to alter nature. With fire we could cook and change the quality and the taste of our food. Fire taught us we could improve our lives and not simply accept a present reality as God's unchangeable will.

Controlling fire was the first step in mankind's progress towards scientific knowledge and technological achievement. The gift from God of fire to Adam and Eve immediately at the conclusion of the divine week of creation was the heavenly way of instructing them that it was now mankind's role to accept a covenant of partnership and to begin the task of human creativity.

We were now empowered to become co-creators.

That is why we make *Havdalah* at the conclusion of every Sabbath – to remind us of the divine gift as well as the responsibility that flows from it.

As we face every new week we need to reflect on God's message when he handed the torch of creativity over to us. He said, "I did whatever I am going to do and I left the world unfinished purposely so that you could complete it. I want you to be a partner with me."

That elevates human beings to a level that is incredible, a level that is divine.

We are to be creative.

How can we be creative? Every person has the obligation to look inside their own self and recognize their unique talents. Their unique talents are God's ways of saying, "This is the way in which you can add to the world's perfection. This is the way you can do something which no one else can." You have been given this gift and talent.

And remember, When you are creative, you are fulfilling your divine mission of becoming a partner with God.

Purpose

Everybody has a life's purpose. The way to realize it is to stop and consider our talents. Our talents are obviously God-given. I was not given the aptitude to hit a ball five hundred feet. I was not given the ability to be a musician. That does not say something negative about me. Rather it means that God did not want my life to develop in that way; He gave me other talents.

In God's infinite wisdom, He did not just hand them to me on a silver platter. He said, "You want to be what you can be? I am going to show you that when you study, you are going to find profound joy in it. When you speak, there are people who are going to say 'that was pretty good.'" But take the pretty good and turn it into a very good. Take your God given talents and develop them so you can make a difference in your lifetime.

That is what it is all about. Everybody has to, by trial and error, intuition, or through the criticisms as well as the applause of others, begin to realize what they are good at.

What are you are good at is God's way of telling you the reason why He put you here on earth.

Controlling the Negative

There is a horse and a jockey. Who is in charge? The jockey is meant to ride the horse. The horse is not meant to ride the jockey.

Negative inclinations come from negative desires. They go back to the fundamental truth of the two drives within us. Given free will, we have an ongoing battle within us between our good and our evil inclinations.

They were created by God for a reason.

They are there to allow us personal growth. Personal growth comes from making the right choices. Personal growth comes from overcoming. Personal growth comes from making the right decisions.

In order to decide correctly we need to define our choices correctly. We need to assess them ethically. We need to be wise enough when necessary to say, "If I do this, this would be wrong" and courageous enough to act in accord with our decision.

Moreover, we need to define our choices by way of their purpose. How will what I propose to do really affect my life? What do I ultimately stand to gain from the choice I propose to make?

So many times people confuse immediate gratification with ultimate goals.

Very often people will justify a particular path on the grounds that it will reward them with more money. If you ask a follow-up question, "Why do you want more money?" the response is seemingly straightforward: I want money to buy a new car. Why do you want to buy a new car? I need it in order to get a better job. Why do you need a better job? Because it pays more money. And so we go around in vicious cycles.

You need to define for yourself *what you really want* and recognize what are the negatives and what are the positives. Then the decisions are really pretty easy.

Dreams

Most of the world thinks that Freud was the first one to have the incredible insight that there is validity to dreams, that dreams have any meaning.

Actually, in Judaism, we were aware of this thousands of years ago, as recorded in the Talmud.

In the pages of this ancient treasure of Jewish tradition the rabbis spoke about dreams and their symbolic meaning. And their discussions were based on references in the Bible, going all the way back to Pharaoh of Egypt, whose dreams were interpreted by Joseph.

Pharaoh dreamt dreams that contained important messages from God. The ability of Joseph to explain them is what saved the Egyptian economy and allowed a Jew to assume a role of prominence second to the King. Joseph was wise enough to know that there are many times when dreams must be taken seriously.

The problem with dreams, as the Talmud tells us, is that we have to differentiate between those meant to reveal divine secrets and those simply reflecting physical responses to previous day's activities. Some dreams aren't God but just food speaking to our subconscious senses; what we ate last night or what we thought of last making an unwanted appearance. If you watched a violent TV program before you went to sleep, which I do not suggest you do, you are going to have a dream that will in some way keep alive the vision of what you just saw. That is bad and that is not prophetic. The Talmud accepts this possibility. Not every dream is meant to be taken seriously.

How do you tell what is prophetic and what is not?

Granted, it is very difficult. But there are times where you see part of a dream being fulfilled. And then you know that God was giving you a mission. There are people who have had visions of their future life's work in dreams. If they are positive, good things in your dreams, then the Rabbis advise you take note of them. If you have an opportunity, *make them come true*. That would be the first step: God implanting the desire or knowledge about these things. If the dreams are bad, there are times when in Jewish law we are told to proclaim a fast or give charity so that something that was a vision in your dream should not come to pass. It was God's warning. It is a very lengthy subject but the bottom line is that dreams must not always be discounted as meaningless.

Money

There is a great *Midrash*, a rabbinic homily, on money.

When God commissioned Moses to count the Jewish people, He told him, "I want you to take half a *shekel* from every Jew and then you will add up the shekels and see how many Jews there are."

The *Midrash* says that Moses was perplexed; he did not understand. So God showed him a coin of fire and then Moses understood.

The *Midrash* does not make sense at first glance. What was so difficult about telling the Jews to give half a *shekel* in order to be counted? And how did seeing a coin of fire resolve Moses' difficulty?

The answer of the Rabbis to the first question is that what caused Moses to be perplexed was his inability to understand God's choice for the method of counting Jews. "We are going to count people by way of money? Money is so material! Is this how we are going to fulfill a *mitzvah* (commandment)? Is money the way people should believe we determine whether they count?"

The objection of Moses seems to have great deal of merit. So God showed him a coin of fire. Fire has a dual property. Fire is the most destructive thing on earth. Fire burns, consumes, and destroys. On the other hand, controlling fire is what made civilization possible. Fire is also the most constructive thing in the world. God was telling Moses something we have to remember about wealth. God, by way of the symbolism of fire, taught us that there is a profound duality implicit in money. Money can corrupt; it can permit lives of dissolution and hedonism. Yet at the same time with money we can build schools, sponsor charitable works, and perform all kinds of incredibly noble deeds.

There are philanthropists and there are wastrels. There are people of great wealth who leave legacies of supreme value to mankind even as there are those whose great fortunes are misused only for personal gratification.

To say money is the root of all evil is in Jewish thought incorrect. Money is the root of evil as well as of blessing. Money is the ultimate duality. Money can be a good. Since it has such a dual power, money is probably one of the greatest tests of people's true character.

There is a great quote attributed to the psychologist Erich Fromm: "Show me a man's checkbook, and I will tell you who he really is."

Show me what you do with your money. Show me what you write out checks for and I'll know everything about you.

Self Worth

It is interesting that when people are asked, "What do you think is the most religious value?", they respond, "I guess it is, 'Love your neighbor as yourself.'"

They do not understand that by having made that statement, they have expressed a profound, psychological truth.

What is the very first requirement that is implicit in loving your neighbor as yourself? You have to love yourself!

Before you love your neighbor, you have to love yourself. If you do not love yourself, how can you love anybody else?

Psychologists will tell you that people who hate others basically hate themselves and they are projecting that hate outwardly. We have an obligation to understand who we are. Self loathing is the product of not living up to your fullest potential. It is not having ambition, not having a drive, not doing anything, and not perfecting yourself.

Self loathing really is the acknowledgement of the soul that you are not living up to the divine within you. What you have to do to alter that perspective is to say to yourself, "I have meaning, I have worth."

How do I know that? Because I am here. If I weren't here, if I didn't have purpose, I wouldn't have been created by God. *My very existence on earth acknowledges my worth.* Therefore, the first step in overcoming a lack of self worth, is finding purpose in life. In fulfilling that purpose, you fulfill yourself. In doing that and finding joy in your life, then and only then can you proceed to the next level of loving your neighbor.

Relationships

Love

Love is the ultimate reality.

Love is what makes life worth living.

Adam was alone and God said, "It is not good for a person to be alone."

Loneliness is defined as the inability to have somebody to love. There are people who think they do not need a love relationship but they end up getting a dog. They need to have some way in which to express love because our need to express love is to be like God. God's definition is love.

We only find happiness when we are in a state of love. Chemically they call it endomorphism. I call it by another word, *Ahava*, the Hebrew for love. It not only makes the world go round but it makes my life meaningful. And the Hebrew word has its source meaning in the words "I will give." To love is to be willing to give a part of yourself to another. The essence of love, true love, is to find greater happiness in our ability to give to another than to receive.

There are two sentences in the Bible that use that Hebrew word for love, *Ahava*: Love God and love your neighbor. Fascinating. These two major sentences that summarize our relationships with God and our fellow man are both sentences that highlight the word love.

The Ten Commandments were given on two tablets. The reason why these ten laws were set on two separate tablets rather than one is to indicate the dual nature of human responsibility. One is to fulfill loving God and one is to fulfill loving your neighbor. When we do not have love, our lives are empty and meaningful.

The English word love sounds almost exactly like the Hebrew word *lev,* which means heart. When our heart stops beating, we are dead. When our heart stops loving, we wish we were dead.

Unconditional Love

I don't believe in unconditional love.

The person who a short while back hacked my identity, stole my e-mail address, ripped off my friends to send him money believing they were helping me in a desperate situation get back home from overseas – he is the kind of person who believes in unconditional love.

When I figured out a way to contact the hacker who caused me so much pain, I wrote him a note telling him he had crossed a very serious line when he involved clergy in his criminal activities. I said that I was certain he would face severe divine punishment. For whatever good it might do, I felt my words might at the very least be a goad to his conscience, if not implant a small measure of fear for the results of his misdeeds.

It took but a few hours after my e-mail went off that incredibly enough I received a response. The thief, the hacker, the Nigerian con man actually answered me!

Yes, he was sorry that he caused me pain, he said. And yes, he too agreed that there is a God and that God is aware of what he did. But, and here was the most remarkable part of his response, he assured me that *God is a God of love who will continue to love him no matter what he does.*

Here in a nutshell, to my mind, is the most powerful proof of the danger implicit in a belief in unconditional love. If evildoers need never fear heavenly retribution they can merrily go on their way content in their knowledge that they have carte blanche from God for their wicked behavior. A God who loves us no matter what we do in the end becomes more than a friend – in fact, for the truly evil, he is an accomplice.

I will not correspond with my hacker anymore. I have said my piece. I know why he is not concerned. But I'm truly grateful that he hasn't really stolen my identity. He hasn't begun to grasp what I know from my Judaic heritage, from my understanding of the Torah, from my conscience and from the depths of my soul: Precisely because God loves me so much He holds me accountable for my actions. In that way He permits me to realize my greatest potential – not simply to *get* but to *earn* His love.

Communication

The Bible tells us that man was created in the image of God. All the commentators wonder, what does that mean? We do not look like God. In what way are wc created in His image?

The answer, according to many Jewish philosophers is that we share the trait of speech with God. Human speech is the way we mirror God.

We have the capacity of godliness because of our ability to share the fruits of our intelligence. We can verbalize what is important to us; we can communicate the truths we discovered and the values we hold dear.

That is a precious gift. That is divine. That is the godliness within us.

Here too, we could take this gift and pervert it. There are people who have not had a conversation their entire lives; they have merely uttered criticisms or stupidities.

A conversation is a sharing of wisdom. A conversation is allowing another person some entry into your soul, into the real you. A conversation is learning by dialoguing.

There is a skill known as the art of conversation. When you call it an art, you are implying that it is something that is artistic, that can be learned and improved. We should think about this and develop the ability to converse. In conversing, we are giving something of ourselves. We are giving the gift of our mind and our *Neshama*, our soul, to another person. That is a wonderful thing. When two people meet in conversation, they are sharing their godliness.

That's probably what Henry Longfellow meant when he said, "A single conversation across the table with a wise man is better than ten years of mere study of books."

Sex

One thing that we happily know as Jews is that in our religion sex is viewed positively as an ultimate good.

For Christians celibacy, surprisingly, was touted as an ideal. I remember seeing a movie many years ago, "Never on Sunday." It got its title from the fact that in Catholic countries on "the Lord's day" sex was considered illegal. Holiness and sexual pleasure were deemed incompatible.

In Judaism sexual relations should always take place on Friday night. As Nachmanides put it, "Let the holy act be performed on the holy night."

It is fascinating to note that in Judaism we call sex holy.

It is holy, if you stop and think about it. A very important way in which we imitate God is by being creators, by having a family. Having children is accomplished through the sexual act. God must have thought a great deal about sex in order to make that the starting point of the biggest mitzvah. He made it so pleasurable because He wanted us to enjoy it. He wanted us to have the happiness it can give and to produce greater love between two people.

What can be a more positive experience than knowing someone as intimately as through sex, an all-consuming, passionate and loving merging of bodies and souls?

That is why in Hebrew the word for "sex" and the word for "knowing" are the same. In the Torah it says, "Adam knew Eve." He knew her because he was intimate with her. To take sex and divorce it from true intimacy is to turn it into a physical act that has no meaning. But sex with true intimacy, which merges not only bodies but souls, is the most beautiful thing in the world.

Spirituality

God's Existence

There are numerous ways in which philosophers have answered the question of proof about the existence of God.

First and foremost there is the concept of design, what theologians describe as the proof of Teleology. When we look at the profound intricacies of the world and its creations it is impossible to imagine that the world could have come into being on its own.

If I would show you this watch and I would say, "It just came into being," you would say, "Come on, it tells time, it has function, it clearly is the product of a watchmaker." "No, no, you do not understand" I would explain, "It took thousands of years but the parts came together in a natural way and eventually you have this watch." You would never believe it.

Take a look at me. Take a look at my eyes. We still do not have a camera that it is as good as our own eyes. We still do not have a computer that can replicate the genius of the human mind.

All of creation proves a Creator.

That is a key way in which we understand God.

There are many more reasons why we believe in God. But if you ask me sincerely the most powerful way in which I know God exists, it is the same way that I know I believe in my own existence. How do I know I am really here? Maybe I am a figment of someone's imagination. I *know* I exist.

The same certainty I have in my own existence, is the same certainty that I have in God's existence. Why? Because I am created in His Image. God is in me. There are countless moments in my life when I feel His presence as strongly as I feel my own. To question His existence is as far-fetched a belief as to question myself.

Finding God

First of all, God is asking the same question. God is looking for you.

You do not have to look very far to find God because God is everywhere. What you have to do is be ready to acknowledge Him.

There are two main ways in which you can open your eyes to His existence. Maimonides and other Jewish philosophers have spoken about this at great length. The two main areas in which God appears are in nature and in our lives.

I just returned from a trip to the Rocky Mountains in Canada. Viewing the magnificence of this earth without believing in God seems to me simply impossible.

Nature includes who we are. Consider any part of our bodies. The more we know about biology and the human body, the more we have to admit that there is a Creator. We are too intricately designed to have come into being by chance.

But there is yet a more direct way in which God makes Himself known. If we only choose to listen well we often have the opportunity to become aware of His presence. In the story of our lives, we can invariably find God if we read the pages carefully.

I've had countless moments where God spoke to me. Today, people would say, "You are crazy. God spoke to you? God does not speak to anybody. The age of the prophets is long gone."

That is not true. God still speaks – in His own way through the language of what some might erroneously call coincidence. When something that is statistically impossible occurs in my life in response to my prayers, that is God talking. When I meet someone I had to meet at precisely that moment by way of a series of unbelievable coincidences, that is God talking. When somebody calls me who I haven't heard from in years to relay a message I needed to know at that very moment while they couldn't explain why they picked precisely that time to get in touch with me, that is God talking.

There is great truth in the saying that "Coincidence is God's way of choosing to remain anonymous."

I would challenge any person to look at countless moments in their lives, events that are completely improbable, and yet deny that they are the result of direction from a higher power. We need to find the courage and wisdom to admit that for much of what happens to us we have to recognize the pen of God as author.

"This happened because God spoke to me." God speaks to all of us. The only requirement is that we have to develop the ear to listen; we need to tune in to the divine frequency. It is a kind of communication in which, just like without a radio, you do not hear all the signals that are in the air. You must tune in to God's channel. And then you will hear Him.

There is yet a third way in which we can become sensitized to God and be able to find Him in addition to His presence in nature and the coincidences of our lives.

That is by reading His book. Learning Torah makes us more aware of divine talk and speech. It sensitizes us to His presence. That is an additional way to find God. Anybody who does those three things cannot miss Him.

Divine revelation and prayer

Some of the most interesting moments in my life were moments that were difficult at the time, that I thought were tragic when they occurred. But in the course of years I recognized that they were, in retrospect, the greatest lessons in my life. They are too personal to discuss publically, but I find those to be great revelations of God because they were God saying to me in retrospect, "You did not understand. You thought I was being cruel to you when I was being kind to you. These are good things that happened."

I feel God via creativity. I think anybody who is creative in any way will tell you, "I do know how I ultimately thought of the ideas I wrote in this book. I do know how I thought of this sermon. I just began and it came into my head." Creativity is God working His way into my soul, so to speak. That is another way in which I recognize God. I could not do this on my own.

The only way you make prayer more powerful is to pray. In other words, it is a skill. It is something you have to do. It is something you should not do with intent for immediate response. When you pray, you are not praying to get something but rather *to be with someone.* When you are praying, you are praying to strengthen the relationship that we spoke of. You are praying, meaning you are with God.

Understanding that relationship helps you recognize that everything that happens in your life has a divine source and therefore you are not troubled. You cannot be afraid when you are with God because God is managing the world. So I am afraid but God will work it out. I cannot be that concerned because I have God on my side.

What you need to do is develop the idea of prayer. That is why people often say, "I do not feel like praying right now" are greatly mistaken. If you only pray when you feel like it, you will not be able to pray. I had some supreme moments in my life of prayer. I was there when my wife gave birth to my son. I was in the room. I felt such holiness and spirituality and I prayed. The only reason I was able to pray then was because I had been praying all my life. That prayer had far greater meaning. Keep praying. Develop the skill. In the moments when it really counts, you will be praying with all of your heart, soul, and mind.

Relationship with God

Having a relationship with God is like having a relationship with a friend. The first thing is you have to be there, you have to talk to Him. Prayer is important not because you are asking God for things and you are going to get them in return. That is ridiculous.

Prayer is a way of acknowledging that you stand in His presence in this world.

Prayer is a way of recognizing that when you use the word "God", you do not mean God as a force, as a concept, as an abstraction, but you mean God as *a personal reality in your life.*

Prayer is a way of proving that you believe you have a personal relationship with God – that you love him and that he in turn loves you.

When I pray, I'm demonstrating my belief that God knows me.

That is incredible since there are billions of people in the world! And yet it is possible for Him to know and to care about me. That is what makes Him God.

God and I have a relationship which needs to be fostered and strengthened. The way to accomplish this is by dialogue. I can talk to Him; that is called prayer. He talks to me; that is called Torah. The two together create our discussions. Then, the more I develop this friendship by speaking to Him and listening to Him, the closer we become. And that strengthens our relationship.

People who are extremely religious because they have spent their lives strengthening their spiritual awareness do not *believe* in God anymore. They *know* God. I am familiar with many people who are on that level. For them, God is a reality.

That should be our goal. Not to believe in God but to achieve a higher level. To know He exists is to turn Him from a fanciful idea into a true friend.

The Soul

The soul is the real me.

There is only one thing in me that has remained a constant.

If you take a look at pictures of me as a child and compare it to the way I look today, you will find very little similarity. Where am "I"? Who is the "I" that is thinking and responding right now? Who is the "me" that stays with me throughout my life and defines my essence?

In Jewish thought, we are created with a soul. It not only defines who I am while I am here on earth, but because it comes from God, it is eternal like God. That is why every human being is immortal. Because we are Godly.

The soul, the *Neshama*, is my essence.

Let me tell you something else about the soul. I disagree with Freud. Freud said: Id, Ego and Superego. He said that deep down we are animalistic. Our real original self is the Id. We need to learn to be controlled by an internal policeman.

I can't concur. Deep inside I am not an Id, I am a *Yid*, I am Jew with a spark of holiness. Every morning I recite the phrase from our tradition that teaches, "My Lord, the soul that you have implanted within me is pure."

Deep down inside of me there is a holy essence, a striving for spirituality and communion with my Creator. Every human being on earth knows it. We call this thirst for godliness by different names - self-expression, self-fulfillment, and self-realization. But all of these are different terms that merely express our awareness of God within us. And that is our soul.

Prayer

Can you imagine the great gift that God gives us by saying, "You can talk to me. I will allow you to speak me" ? And not only that, "I will listen." God says, "I hear you."

I am not just a little dot in the universe. I am important to God. When I talk to God and know that my life has meaning to Him, it has meaning to me. Most people think of prayer as giving God a list of the things they need. That is not what prayer is. Prayer is a relationship. Imagine if a relationship with a friend is predicated only on what you can get out of him. God is so close to me that I want to talk to Him and in talking to Him, three times a day, I become a better person.

What a great gift! Whether He makes me win the lottery or not, prayer fulfills what I need most, a friend on high.

If you do not practice playing the piano, you will never have the peak moments. If you do not practice playing basketball, you will never be in the zone. If you do not continue to pray on a regular basis, you cut off the relationship. There was a peak moment when my wife gave birth. I was there when my son was born. I walked into the room and made a blessing the likes I had never made before. I thanked God for letting me see this day. This was a peak spiritual moment. But the reason why I was able to pray was because for so long I had created this closeness with God that I felt it very easy to open up my mouth and say what had to be said then.

The Sabbath

The Sabbath is one of the Ten Commandments. The Sabbath is the key to our weekly re-spiritualization. Six days a week we work. We work because we have to. That is fulfilling the needs of our body. But your soul is just as important. Your soul needs to be recharged spirituality.

Those who misunderstand the Sabbath, think it is meant primarily as a day of rest. You worked for six days. Therefore, on the seventh day, go to sleep. It is absurd. If someone were to sleep through the entire Sabbath, they would miss the entire meaning. The Sabbath is the day in which you say six days I am working because I have to. I have to eat. I have to be alive. Physically I need to. The seventh day is the day to step back and say, "Why am I really doing this?" Every seventh day is a day in which we get on the couch, not to rest, but to do our own psychological introspection as we say to ourselves, "Who am I? Why am I here on earth? What is my purpose?" In turning the Sabbath into a day that is filled with spiritual activities, a day of prayer, study, being with family, reaffirming love, and connecting again with those that are most meaningful to you, you are re-defining and re-sanctifying your life every seventh day.

I am a Jew

I have to be one of the luckiest people in the world. If you ask billions of people in the world, who are Christians or Muslims, "What is the source of your religion?" They will tell you it all goes back to the Five Books of Moses, to the Torah. I am someone who is privileged to be amongst the people born into Judaism who represent the beginning of all moral teachings, ethics, and Godly wisdom. That has been transmitted, we believe, from God to Moses at Sinai. We have never diluted the product. We have the original. We have survived in ways that are miraculous.

King Louis XIV asked Pascal, "Do you believe in miracles?" He answered, "Yes." "Well" said the king, "Tell me one miracle." He said, "The Jewish people, your majesty." We are a miracle. Our survival is a miracle. What we have achieved is miraculous. What we represent is what in fact the prophets said: We are a light unto the nations. I want to be part of that light.

I pray that you too will find the kind of joy my faith has given me.

About the Author

Rabbi Benjamin Blech is an internationally recognized educator, religious leader, author, and lecturer.

Rabbi Blech is the author of twelve highly acclaimed and best selling books, with combined sales of close to half a million copies, including three as part of the highly popular Idiot's Guide series. His book, *Understanding Judaism: The Basics of Deed and Creed*, was chosen by the Union of Orthodox Jewish Congregations as "the single best book on Judaism in our generation". Together with an accompanying six hour video, filmed by the producers of 20/20, featuring Rabbi Blech, it is presently being used as the basis for study groups in numerous synagogues and universities around the country.

His book *Taking Stock: A Spiritual Guide To Rising Above Life's Financial Ups and Downs* was featured in a full page article in the Sunday *New York Times* and one of his recent works, *If God is Good, Why Is The World So Bad?* has been translated into Indonesian where it has had a powerful reception in the wake of the country's tsunami, as well as into Portuguese.

In a national survey, Rabbi Blech was ranked #16 in a listing of the 50 most influential Jews in America.

A recipient of the American Educator of the Year

Award, he is a Professor of Talmud at Yeshiva University since 1966 and has formed thousands of student-teacher relationships through his warm and caring style.

A tenth-generation rabbi, Rabbi Blech is Rabbi Emeritus of Young Israel of Oceanside, which he served for 37 years.

He is a frequent lecturer in Jewish communities as far-flung as Australia, South Africa, New Zealand, Bangkok, Singapore, Hong Kong, Tokyo and Israel. Closer to home, he has served as Scholar-in-Residence at hundreds of synagogues throughout the United States and Canada and been active on behalf of countless Jewish causes.

His lectures on tape have an international following and are among the most popular from among the thousands made available on the web through Aish Hatorah. He is known for his ability to present complicated ideas in a clear and entertaining manner.

A past President of both the National Council of Young Israel Rabbis, as well as the International League for the Repatriation of Russian Jewry, Rabbi Blech has also served as officer for the New York Board of Rabbis as well as the Rabbinical Council of America.

He has appeared on national television (including the Oprah Winfrey Show); hosted a popular weekly radio program in New York; and written for *Newsweek, The*

New York Times and *Newsday*, in addition to a wide and varied number of scholarly publications.

As a result of his personal meeting with the late Pope John Paul II, he was instrumental in securing the loan of precious Jewish manuscripts for exhibition in Israel and he is presently involved in further negotiations for the return of precious Judaica held by the Vatican that may well prove to be of historic significance.

Rabbi Blech is an unusually eloquent and gifted speaker, as well as a profound contemporary theologian and religious spokesman, who has made a major impact on the many tens of thousands of people he has addressed.

AND MOST RECENTLY:

Rabbi Blech's latest book, which was published in April 2008, was featured on *Nightline, Good Morning America* and a one-hour special on *20/20.*

The Sistine Chapel: Michelangelo's Forbidden Messages in the Heart of the Vatican

Coinciding with the 500th anniversary of Michelangelo's starting work on the frescoes of the Sistine Chapel, this groundbreaking book is already the subject of huge interest, discussion and controversy. Translated into 15 languages, including Japanese, available in 25 countries, a first printing of 100,000 copies by HarperOne, movie and TV rights presently in negotiation with three major film companies, and national TV coverage, this major work proves that Michelangelo incorporated many teachings of Jewish Midrash and Kabbalah into the Sistine Chapel – daring ideas unknown to its 4 million annual visitors. And unlike the DaVinci Code, this book is not fiction but fact. Enrico Bruschini, official Art Historian of the American Embassy in Rome, in his Foreword to the book writes, "Just as the work of Michelangelo in the Sistine Chapel changed forever the world of art, so will this book change forever the way to view and, above all, to understand the work of Michelangelo!"

About Sinai Live Books

 Sinai Live is committed to assisting high-quality teachers share their wisdom. Our goal is to enhance our readers' personal Jewish journeys and elevate everyday life through thoughtful and insightful content. We aim to engage, inspire and encourage further exploration.

Our books include:

 Telushkinisms: Wisdom to the Point
by Rabbi Joseph Telushkin

 *Footsteps: Perspectives on Daily Life*
by Rebbetzin Esther Jungreis

 Passport to Kabbalah: A Journey of Inner Transformation
by Rabbi DovBer Pinson

Visit www.sinailive.com or contact us at info@sinailive.com to learn more.

About Rethink Partners

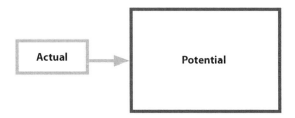

This reading experience was developed by Mark Pearlman's Rethink Partners, an organization dedicated to shifting user and industry perspectives through a combination of business strategy, product management, sales and marketing, editorial, design and online implementation.

Rethink Partners works with for-profit and non-profit organizations to help them reach their potential. We are focused on seeing both what is and what could be.

Visit us at www.rethinkpartners.com.

Acknowledgements

This book would not have been possible without the help of many people. Special thanks goes to:

Mark Pearlman, for documenting the Rabbi Blech and other world-class teachings on video over the past decade, for helping hundreds of thousands of people access these lectures at events and on the Internet through Sinai Live and JInsider, and for his initiative to create and publish this unique book.

Jake Laub, for his creativity in design and diligence in editing.

Raquel Amram, for her meticulous transcriptions and editing.

Daniel Schanler, for his expertise in video editing and production.

Made in the USA
San Bernardino, CA
11 September 2013